When Love Hurts and Wins

Toyin Fajinmi

Order this book online at www.trafford.com
or email orders@trafford.com

Most Trafford titles are also available at major online book retailers.

Printed in the United States of America.

ISBN: 978-1-4669-4347-6 (sc)
ISBN: 978-1-4669-4346-9 (e)

Trafford rev. 07/16/2012

 www.trafford.com

North America & international
toll-free: 1 888 232 4444 (USA & Canada)
phone: 250 383 6864 ♦ fax: 812 355 4082

Contents

Dedication

This book is dedicated to my beautiful wife for her continual support, enthusiasm, and love. Also to my amazing children Tolu and Tobi, who keeps me happy and loved.

Appreciation

$\mathcal{M}$y sincere appreciation goes to my cousin Yinka who was an enormous support in so many ways to make this dream a reality.

What Is Marriage?

- Marriage is the unity of two imperfect individuals

- Marriage is love without reservations or limitations

- Marriage is always new

- Marriage is the rebirth of a new day

- Marriage is the beginning of a new life

- Marriage is a union ordained and initiated in heaven

- Marriage is like tongue and teeth, which at times, have differences but compliments one another

- Marriage is understanding one another

- Marriage is acceptance of imperfections and support for one another

- Marriage is about falling in love with love itself

- Marriage is agreement in love and disagreement on life issues with love

- Marriage is about having one's partner's interests at heart at all times

- Marriage is about total surrender without expectations

- Marriage is the son of commitment and grandson of love

- Marriage is like a piggybank, you get what you invest if it is not stolen from you

- Marriage is another life as it is planned

- Marriage endures test, trials, and tribulations by the grace of God

- Marriage is a pledge to love, to hold, and to cherish

- Marriage is an ageless vow

- Marriage is what you make it to be and not a mistake

- Marriage is finding that one person in a billion

- Marriage is fulfillment of dreams

- Marriage is the acceptance of your partner's shortcomings

- Marriage is consummation of love and a stamp of reality to dating

Selection of a Partner

$\mathcal{S}$election of a partner can be difficult, and it varies with culture and society. Choosing a partner is very complex from daily restlessness of uncertainties, to thinking about family acceptance of the chosen individual. Acceptance of people can sometimes be an issue in many cultures. Some families are still in control of who the children marry, the race of the person, or the region the person comes from because of experiences or history.

Looking around the world in this new age, I can say confidently that love is no longer the basis for selecting a spouse or partner. When love is secondary, physical attraction is mostly the "key" in terms of body physique, especially facial appearance and good looks are usually the point of focus. What is considered attractive in one culture and society may not be desirable in another. Like the common adage that says "beauty is in the eyes of the beholder," people around the world have different views and opinions about beauty. Some African societies consider thick (big) women to be attractive whereas in the western culture, heavy set women are usually labeled unhealthy. Physical appearance based on individual preferences varies for instance, the type of body shape desired in today's society may not be considered thick enough to be attractive in comparison to few decades ago. Education and wealth are also important in partner selection criteria in many societies and these sometimes are more important than physical appearances.

Are these characteristics important enough and can they bring love to you or make you happy in a marriage? Does anyone's opinion matter when choosing a partner other than your own? These are important questions to ask yourself when you are in the process of selecting a partner. Love is the emotions felt for someone else, the willingness to lose oneself for the sake of the other person, letting go of everything just to satisfy the other person, tolerating one another and acceptance of the other person's shortcomings. Getting married to someone who is not physically attractive to you will not be a good idea but has worked for some people, which makes physical attraction invalid. The proven result from countries, such as Pakistan and some parts of India have shown that arranged marriages regardless of physical attractions can and do result in long-lasting marriages if both party involved are willing to invest time, emotions, and dedication.

People in the Western world often argue that arranged marriages are old-fashioned and a take away from women the right to choose who she wants to be with or spend her life with. However; considering the divorce rate of marriages in the "civilized countries" on the other hand, one will rather choose a long-lasting family assured through the arranged marriage as compared to the coin flipping marriages of today. Young people seem to be focused on wrong quality that will not bring fort lasting union. For instance, today's youth focus more attention on "beauty" and neglect other important qualities. Family values, individual values, and the fear of God are very important attributes to assess in prospective partners. A man raised with the value that 'women are "lesser being," 'second citizens, and "suppose to serve men" will likely not treat a woman with respect. A man who believes in hitting or beating on women to gain respect as superior will likely beat on his wife and a man who does not believe in God Almighty definitely will not support the wish of his wife to serve God and vice versa.

Selecting a life partner is a delicate issue that needs to be handled with caution. People needs better understanding about relationships along with divine intervention to make a good choice for a long-lasting union because good and strong marriages are the backbones of the society. Thinking it through before making a decision, not to focus on looks and financial benefits and to ask God for guidance is the key to choosing a partner because marriage is not like goods that can be returned to the departmental stores after a defect is detected.

Love and Marriage

$\mathcal{M}$arriage as defined in universal language is a union between a man and a woman, from the onset of creation according to the holy books and even from stone age as it was told in human history. Marriage in this new generation has come with different meaning and understanding of the popular phrase "for better for worse" as it is generally understood by the populace that no matter what life throws in your path as partners, no matter how good or bad things are, be it emotional, physical, financial stability or instability, the two will "stick" together and work through it.

Marriages in history have come in different ways starting from men working as a core man to marry his master's daughter, arranged marriages that are still in practice in some cultures around the world, and the latest in vogue of 'I found, I bring marriages' have its pros and cons outcomes just like most marriages in history. Many cultures have paid "bride prices"; have given to a woman or her family in exchange for sexual access. Many societies have different practices about marriages; some cultures frown at men with more than one wife therefore; only monogamy is lawful. An example is the United States whereas some cultures encourage men to have more than one wife under the same roof or outside the home, which is considered polygamy. Marriages have been hindered and controlled by culture, religion, age, and social groups. Some societies have shifted slightly from the traditional man and woman marriages to allow same sex unions. In what ever direction your marriage is heading, it is an agreement between two people to come together to share similar views, reach compromised conclusions, share love, and emotions with one another with one question in mind-till WHEN?

The popular phrase mentioned earlier "till death do us part," have shed other meanings, which makes one wonder if the phrase needs to be changed, re-phrased, or erased from marriage vows. This phrase as I have learned from many couples is just like any other word without second thoughts of what it means and no other meaning except that it is a part of the popular marriage vows.

Death as some have claimed could be when the marriage is financially dead, when it becomes difficult to make ends meet, loss of job, inability to support spouse or to satisfy financial obligations. Emotional death as many couples believe, is when people lose feelings for spouse because of infidelity or lack of communication. Therefore, "death in marriage" is interpreted by many people in different ways and not necessary the physical death of the spouse as it was meant in the "vows." The understanding of "till death do us part" as physical, financial, or emotional death cannot be measured or compared in whatever way people prefer to selfishly interpret the phrase for personal gain.

Marriage is tagged to be a long-term dating relationship contract and the institution of marriage is a mere joke in today's society. Marriage is a good thing that comes with many benefits, be it financial, companionship, intimacy, pro-creation, or just having someone to come home and chat with on the happenings of the day. Marriage also has its challenging moments of arguments, selfishness, lies, deceits, and heart breaks. Marriage is not a union in which people can chose to accept the "good times" and reject the "challenges" but with a good understanding, the scale can be balanced out resulting in a positive outcome.

Communication and Marriage

$\mathcal{C}$ommunication is the binder that holds a relationship together and if the binder breaks, the papers will start to fall off. When spouses no longer communicate, the marriage nurtures no one, and it is no longer a marriage. Effective communication is very important in any relationship, especially in a marriage as couples climb the ladder of life together. Communication lines have to be open and each partner is equipped with equal right of expression. Marriage communication requires energy and understanding putting aside personal feelings and views while communicating with spouse. There are some key issues that need to be addressed when one person is trying to communicate with his or her partner.

Respect is the key when communicating with your partner:

- Refrain from talking over your spouse.

- Be respectful of your spouse's opinion even if you disagree, do not challenge his or her suggestions.

- Show interest in the conversation.

- Express thoughts and do not be judgmental of your spouse's opinion.

- Encourage your partner to be part of the conversation without being controlling.

- Clarify everything you say and ask for clarification on what you do not understand. Do not assume.

- Do not show dislike for what your spouse has to say.

- Do not interrupt your spouse even if what he or she says is unpleasant.

- Remember that you are still communicating even when you are not talking be aware of your facial expression and body language.

Communication is important and do not rely on intuition. Spouses genuinely assume their spouse could read their minds and fail to communicate effectively. Many people tend to think for their spouse and believe they will understand their thoughts. This leads to argument or making the wrong decisions that may have been avoided if good communication was in practice. A good communication is an effective way to achieve a true marital bond.

➢ Be focused on the issue.

➢ Do not talk down on your partner during discussions.

➢ Compromise is important when trying to solve marital problems and if you cannot reach a decision make sure you end your conversation on a positive note.

> Do not lose track of your conversation. Focus on one thing at a time and refrain from jumping to other issues until one is resolved.

> It is not good to get a third party involved in your marriage but if you need to, use wisdom to determine when an outside help is needed like, a marriage counselor and preferably a respectable married pastor or clergyman.

Good communication is a skill that anyone can learn and it involves both partners' commitments. Many couples did not experience communication problem while dating and when they get hit with their first communication breakdown due to unrealistic expectations of marriage they become disappointed. Realistically men and women communicate differently, and it is no surprise why communication can be challenging sometimes. Men communicate to solve problems whereas women communicate to make emotional connections, which spells out why men are more physical and women are emotional. Men and women need to communicate effectively their wants and needs in a non-threatening manner.

Be honest with your spouse, express your feelings, and share thoughts. Honesty should be exercised with caution and apply wisdom when communicating with your spouse. Remember, words are like air when spoken, it is impossible to retrieve and recall. Do not remove God's given filter between your mouth and the brain. Always remember that your spouse has feelings and do not dish out what you cannot take. Honesty and love enhance effective communication. Communication is the ability to hear, digest, and handle the message with maturity. Marriage is a lifelong journey and if you both love each other as you claim to, let your line of communication be the sparkle light that will light up your romance.

Distractions in Marriages

$\mathcal{M}$arriage is a union, and a bond between two people coming together to share love, likeness, and differences for a common goal of growing together as one. The general idea of what marriage ought to be is ideal, but with busy lives, children involvements, and other engagements, people tend to grow further and farther apart daily in marriages. Recognizing and realizing distractions in marriages is the first step to dealing with and resolving the issues created by distractions. Some distractions can be corrected and amendments could be made right away like finding baby sitters to take care of the children while the couples spend time together. Other distractions require deep thoughts and planning to resolve as in the case of employments.

What are some of these marriage distractions?

- Children: Having children is a norm in societies and children are definitely amazing to have. They are a part of our daily family lives with special priority and attention to their needs and wants. Children involvement sometimes makes people to forget who they are because of several responsibilities that children demand from parents. These demands varies from changing diapers, making meals, attending PTA meetings at school, helping with homework, preparing for the following school day, eating dinner, and enforcing early bedtime as part of daily routine as parents. Taking care of children will take up so much of your time that you and your spouse will hardly have a spare time to spend together and at times, this becomes overwhelming to the point of letting go of your own interests and unconsciously neglecting your spouse in the process. This is especially common but not restricted to women. If caring for children is keeping you and your spouse from enjoying each other, it is time to devise a plan to save your marriage. Find a trusted family member or friend to watch the children and plan a getaway night with each other. Hold hands, go to dinner, go to the movies, walk in the park, look each other in the eyes, and remind yourselves how much you love, miss, and appreciate one another. It is not advisable to have the isolated romantic time-out only once in a while however; try to make it a practice to spend time together without distractions as often as possible.

- Employment and Career Involvement: Work takes us away from home and uses most of our hours daily. Having a job is good as it provides us with the means to care for our family. Balancing work and family life with your spouse can be a little bit challenging for many couples. Taking your work home at the end of the day is a habit most people practice and employers are not making things easier as they expect you to do more daily than what you get paid for. It can be difficult not to think about your job while at home as most of us are striving to get better in our place of employments. Many people must work harder to be recognized and rewarded for what we do daily for performance enhancements and to stay well above the water. Many have to work much harder than others to prove themselves at their respective jobs and some have to work twice as hard to get recognized and promoted for a better compensation or to increase what they bring home in their paychecks. Planning and having time alone with your spouse is sometimes easier to say than in reality. Many people would want time with their spouse but the work stress travel home with them.

Working hard is good and being an excellent employee is fantastic however; that should not be an excuse to neglect your responsibilities over your children and your spouse. Jobs will come and go as you may secure a job today and get dismissed tomorrow but your family will not always be the same, and they will always need you. Children grow-up faster than you think and the time you missed in their lives cannot be gained back. Your spouse will stick with you through thick and thin even without a job and the memories of quality time spent together will sustain the family. Remember, people are replaceable at work but never at home with your family. You are a unique person with special traits that only you possess, and you are the most valued and the very important person in your family. Creating a precious time with your spouse is crucial in a marriage and your job may be the distraction creating a barrier between you and your spouse from growing in your marriage. Changing jobs might be essential if the current job does not leave a room for you and your spouse because finding a new job is much easier and faster than finding a spouse in a lifetime who is willing to love, care, and grow old with you.

Most jobs are good to you anyway if you possess certain skills and abilities. The job cares when you are full of energy and can move the organization forward but does not want to grow old with you because you will become a liability. Most employments are about profit

making and are ready to get rid of you after many years
of tireless service before you are struck with old age
related medical issues. Your family will not abandon
you like some jobs will.

Relationships: Many relationships come in different ways and
can be in form of old friends, old lovers, families, or friends.
Old lovers' involvement or reconciliation is the number one
distraction in this category. Many are quick to run to their old
boy or girl friends for advice concerning his or her marriage.
Exes are labeled "ex" for a reason and that line of friendship
with your "ex" should not be crossed again. "Exes" are people
that you either used to date or were involved with and so
they will likely know your weaknesses and strengths. This
person knows your likes and dislikes, knows what to tell you
or share with you to make you feel that you are at a loss for
not being with him or her, and to destroy your relationship.
They will tell you how much positive things have transpired
in their own lives because you left and tell you lie after lies
to further disorganize your mind. Soon you will start to doubt
your love for your current partner, even comparing him or
her to your "ex." Distraction sets in and with a divided and
disoriented mind you start making plans for possible re-union.
Regrets of your relationship will start to surface, bond with
current partner starts to loosen, and things begin to fall apart.
Remember, he or she is the" EX" for a reason best known to
you and just as a leopard never changes his spots, an "EX" will
come to you as a changed and reformed person but his or her
mind is like a chameleon trying to deceive you and make you
go astray. Let "by-gone be by-gone" and remember, you look
radiant because God and your partner make you happy. Some
old friends are sometimes better than new ones because old
friends knew you when you were nobody. Having relationship
with positive old friends is encouraged but those friends
without positive attitudes and who do not support your family
values can be distractions to a marriage. They are quick to let

you know how much you are missing-out by not associating with your old group and are quick to compare your spouse to your old friends or lovers. "Staying away from distractions" and this could mean family, new friends, and neighbors. Such people can only interfere in your relationship as much as you allow them because you hold the staff of office, and the ball is in your court. You alone can determine how much involvement you want in your relationship and letting families know that your role has changed either as a spouse or parent may be the right thing to say to keep distraction away from your family.

Marriage or Partner Comparison: Comparison of marriage or partners is a distraction that sneaks in your mind and continues to grow with the potential to cause damage in your relationship. Be mindful that your spouse is a unique person with different lifestyle. "Fingers are not created equal" and so your spouse is an individual with a special mind. Many will lie about how much their spouse does for them to make their marriage look better than yours. Some will dine at a fast food restaurant and tell you lies that he or she just left a soul and exotic restaurant with the spouse just to distract your mind and compare your marriage to theirs. They will be quick to tell you how much their spouse earns and how fortunate they are as they have been showered with expensive gifts. Many will tell you untrue stories and if you are not endowed with the wisdom of God, you will start to wonder why you are so unlucky not to have a spouse like theirs. Remember, "Not all that glitters is gold," and it is better to be hungry but happy than to have exotic foods and be showered with expensive gifts; yet unhappy.

Distractions are always present in marriages however; timely recognition and resolution of the issues will help sustain the love shared and help the couple grow in a marriage.

Sex and Marriage

$\mathcal{S}$ex in marriage is a good, beautiful, and sacred thing that defines the deepest level of involvement, sharing, and intimacy that you and your spouse can share. Many people have false perception of sex in a marriage and have developed a false belief based on negative information. Sex can be breathtaking if shared in love however; it can result in the downfall of a marriage if close attention is not paid to it. Sex is the highest physical way of sharing or expressing one's love and affection to his or her partner.

Sex is also an act that you do not want to deprive your partner of. It is a marital right shared willingly and in a loving affectionate manner. Making love is an endless act that spells out the security of being in a loving union. Sex should not be forced, perform aggressively to hurt the other partner, conducted in a way that creates fear in the other person or with intimidation by any of the partners. Lovemaking is an important sub-division of a marriage so sacred and is the traditional way of procreation. A new life springs from sex and it is meant to be enjoyed mutually by both partners not just by one of the couple. When sex becomes a routine in a marriage, boredom kicks in, and other insignificant problems will start crawling into the marriage. Sex is a loving and affectionate bond between married couples and a good way of satisfying one another when your bodies call out for each other. When you long for your spouse, the "goose spots" become visible when in each other's arms, thus your sex life is rising in a positive direction. The passionate connection of partners when in love cannot be described much less the feelings of getting lost in each other's arms.

Sex is a vital part of any marriage but in the ancient times, people did not like to discuss it. Couples at that time did not share each other's desire openly and those courageous enough to express theirs were labeled as been "promiscuous." As such partners were secretive about their desires and wants when it came to lovemaking as most people would prefer to refer to the act. Some have defined sex as the act of just penetration or the willingness to satisfy one's partner and ignore self needs while "love making" is the passionate act of both partners to satisfy each other through a sexual bond. The separation of facts from myths is essential during sex discussion with your partner because it can strengthen or destroy a marriage. Expressing your love and care to your spouse through action and intimacy will speak volumes.

Communication about sexual fantasies and desires are important and a good way to spice up your sex life in marriages. Never be intimidated to talk to your spouse about how well you are either satisfied or displeased about your sex life. Communication will improve your sex life than sex toys or expensive sexy lingerie. If you suspect minor sexual problems such as dry vagina, inability to maintain erection, or ejaculation and you know that your loss in sexual desire with your partner is not due to pornography, infidelity, or dependence on sex toys; you need to seek medical professional advice before it is too late. Remember "if you do not use it, you lose it." Keeping your body alert for sexual pleasure with exercise, balanced diet, and engaging in mind challenging activities such as reading and family times will keep you coming back for more. This will enhance your sex life and strengthen your marriage. Exploring new ideas about sex together with your spouse will fill your minds with exciting imaginations. Stop the century long "missionary way" and find comfortable and desirable sexual positions for the two of you to explore and enjoy.

Sex, love making, or intimacy as people refer to it, is not meant for bedroom only but can be enjoyed during the day, mid-day, early evening, and anytime of the night as opposed to late night or early morning that has been traditionally restricted to. Couples may try having sex in any room in the house with respect and consideration for the people around you. It could be in the kitchen but remember to be cautious of utensils and hot surfaces or in the dining room with special attention to unstable diner chairs and tables. Sex in the shower also can be pleasurable with warm or cold shower running down on you while having a blast. Having sex on top of the kitchen counter, on the floor, or anywhere around the house could be very romantic and leave a long-lasting memory in your marriage. The amount of work, fun, excitement, and affection you invest in your sexual life will either enhance or inhibit your intimacy toward one another.

Children in Marriages

𝒞hildren are special gifts from God and a blessing to human race for continuation of life. Children are the products of two unions and a blessing to have. Having children is the expectation of many couples after the knot is tied but how many couples are ready for the responsibilities that follow is a valuable question to ask. The society's expectation of the newlywed sometimes overshadows the couples' plans as pressure mounts from left and right, directing the newlywed in their union.

In many cultures, society often labels women without children after about four or more years of marriage, as "barren" or presume there is problem with the woman. Women looking to God for a blessing of the "womb" are undervalued in many cultures, not less women who have medical problems are considered "unnatural." The amount of pressure impose upon newlywed can give way to stress in their lives and even prevent having viable pregnancies. Many culture and societies around the world are guilty of faulting women when there is delay in their expectation concerning child bearing after marriage. Women are also subjected to double standard concerning delay in child bearing. Many societies fail to view the man as a possible cause of delay instead the woman or the wife as we may say becomes "unwomanly."

The stigmas that women get in marriages are enormous as many go through "hell" with in-laws, friends, and even neighbors. Many people in today's societies view childless women as being punished for either being too promiscuous in her younger years or having too many abortions. In reality, most women with child bearing problems can count in one hand how many men she has been involved with before marriage and some of these women have not for once had any abortion. The society is so judgmental in what the women deal with individually and pre-marital lifestyle may not have any connection with the present situation of inability to conceive.

Many cultures are biased when a woman bears only female children in marriages. Some mothers are not appreciated because they fail to give birth to male children in our gender superior society. Many believe that having a male child is a pride to his or her family, a boost to manhood, and the family name will be carried on. It is a shame that some women have been brainwashed to believe that it is her fault that she could not give birth to male children. Science has proven that men determine the sex of the children and in the Christendom; God determines what a couple will have. Regardless if you have a boy or girl, having healthy children ought to be the paramount concern to parents to live a healthy lifestyle. There is no life continuation without girls and boys and no matter how we look at it one sex is not more significant than the other. In all honesty, having children is an amazing thing because it is an opportunity to love someone, care, and provide for a new offspring, and this opportunity is sometimes not extended to everyone.

Society has forgotten that being childless is not a curse and the inability to conceive could be due to a minor medical problem called "infertility" that may be corrected with very little medical intervention. We are fortunate with how advanced medical breakthrough have gone in this age. We live in a society that believes in "smooth-running" life and are not prepared to deal with the rough roads of life. Infertility is a condition that affects both men and women, preventing them from having children. Some infertility can be corrected with simple medical treatment whereas some may need to be corrected with extensive medical treatments. Man can be affected just as woman, but most people will not look at the man as a possible cause of childlessness because it is the woman who carries the womb. Inaccurate timing for sexual intimacy may also be another factor, while stress due to the daily activities of life can also contribute to the inability to conceive on both parts. Women get hit with most of the blame while the ignorance of family and close friends add to it. Lack of understanding and unwillingness to learn or should I say "male ego" usually prevent many from seeking professional help. Many believe as long as a man can produce sperm during intercourse and as long as a woman has her menstrual period, everything should be fine. Modern medicine has proven that most childlessness is due to some sort of infertility that may be from the male or female. While all attentions are on the women, some men shoot blank, meaning that their sperm contains no life cell, some sperm are low, and some sperm are swimming backward instead of forward. All these male issues can contribute to childlessness in which women are blamed for. Remember that effective communication and togetherness work together for the benefit of the couple when knowledgeable actions are taken.

Having children will not bring happiness to your marriage if you are not already happy, and it is not also good for the development of children to grow in a loveless marriage. Children will make your love stronger only if the love already exist in the marriage and children will be happier in a home filled with love. Children are good to have if you can care for them and show them the true love of God. Paying excessive attention more than necessary to children will also wear out the passion between couples. Couples should take some time out for themselves to go out occasionally on a romantic dinner or vacation without the children interference in order to keep the flame of love in their marriages burning.

Having children because it is the norm is not good and if it is not what you planned or are prepared for will only destroy the foundation and future of those children based on what they see and witness in the marriage. Children can turn a marriage either into a desired or a decayed relationship.

Money and Marriage

$\mathcal{M}$arriage is usually the desired result of romance while people get married for several reasons; financial union is the core reason for marriages. Money and its value are very important in any marriage as romance is vital to a successful union. Things mostly needed in life come down to money such as how much we earn, spend, or save. Making money choices as a team is one important way of preserving a marriage. Understanding each other concerning money issue will alleviate thoughts of financial problems. Financial issues are the reasons for many divorces, and there is no right way for couples to manage their finances but there are many wrong ways if caution is not taken. Money is a good thing to have however; it can destroy a good relationship, especially if you do not have enough of it.

Money issue is one thing lovers do not discuss before saying "I DO," and it is the center-point of any relationship if it is not well planned for. Money can either enhance or destroy a relationship, depending on the adequate planning invested in it. When young people meet and show affection toward each other, many discussions are recommended to determine if you are making the right choice or making a lifetime mistake. People avoid discussions about money because of the fear of negative feedbacks from the other person. It is a good topic to initiate and intensively discuss to prevent future misery. It is wise to know what you are getting into and plan accordingly because your partner may be a "don't ask, don't tell" person. When you fail to ask the necessary questions just because you are afraid that your partner will become angry; it is time to sit back and reconsider if he or she is the right person for you. Having freedom and ability to communicate with your partner in a relationship is a key factor therefore; there should be freedom to express what you want for your future without condemnation. When you fail to plan; you are planning to fail. This is a magic phrase applicable in money and marriage because discussion about money alone is not enough but also to have a plan in place.

As mentioned earlier, there is no right way but many wrong ways to deal with money problems. Many couples have obviously chosen wrong ways with the mind of togetherness but different financial goals. For instance, maintaining separate bank accounts without the other partner's knowledge of the bank's existence may create trust issues in the marriage. Maintenance of a financial separation without accountability or collaboration among married couples may be detrimental to the relationship. Having secrets such as separate financial obligations, plan, and division with money will not help your marriage. The notion of "united we are but divided we bank" is a wrong approach. Couples need to realize that when you are in a marital relationship, there is no longer "me," it is not your money; it is not mine but "ours." No more individualism but collectiveness and understanding.

Here are some tips for the dating couple:

- Know the amount of debt your "soon to be" partner owes and decide if you want to inherit his or her debt. If your partner has too much debt, you can decide on either clearing it before you get married or decide on a plan on how to pay the debt off.

- Be honest because honesty is a vital key in a relationship. Honesty and trust will save your union and being honest with your partner will pay off in the long-run. It may be a very difficult conversation to have but if you approach it with caution and sensitivity, you will not go wrong.

- There are good and bad debts, and it is always a good idea to determine if your partner's debt is a "good" or "luxury debt." A good debt are those debts that result from necessities like mortgages, student loans, and car loans. Long-term loans have good outcome if well planned and these are usually considered good loans because of the benefits.

Bad debts are debt acquired out of luxury not necessities like buying expensive car to show-off, high credit card debts, borrowing money to foot a vacation, irresponsible habit that accumulate debts with high interest rates, and buying unnecessary items to drive up store credit cards. It is advisable to lay everything out on the table and plan accordingly on how to pay or reduce the bad debts because it will not automatically go away. It will make sense to plan ahead than dealing with it after you have been married.

Married Couple

Respect each other's opinion regarding spending, and remember that once married; you become a team. Communication and understanding is vital in a relationship regarding spending issues and coming to a reasonable compromise will definitely help. As we grow older, our needs and wants change therefore; respecting your partner's opinion should matter more.

Communication

Communication and understanding is the key in financial issues. Keep the lines of communication open and make sure you keep the line of communication open about money issues to reduce or eliminate misunderstanding in your marriage.

Bank Accounts

Keeping a joint account works well for some and does not for others. It is important for couples to work out a good plan regarding bank accounts. Having separate accounts does not necessary mean more problems depending on the maturity of the couple, and the reason behind keeping separate account. Does one partner decide to have a separate account to prevent his or her partner from knowing how much he or she has, earns or is it because one partner does not trust the other due to free-spending or extravagant lifestyle.

Budget

It is good to be financially responsible however; tracking your spending is not to be a watch-dog to your partner, but to be a check when things may seem not to be going well financially. It is good to set financial goals when you are both on the same boat.

Financial Secrets

Keeping secrets on purchases can result in loss of confidence in one another if your spouse discovers the secrets, and this can be the genesis of the end to a marriage. Regardless of how difficult it is; always tell the truth.

Financial Decisions

Make informed financial decisions together even if you bring more money to the table. Remember that each of you is in the marriage together and need to involve your partner in any financial decision regardless of how small or big the decision is. This is because if your decision turns out not to be good or ends in a loss, you are in it together. Your debt is hers and hers is yours and if you have good financial times together, you will have to face tough times together financially. Money is a big factor in marriage and when the line of communication is broken, especially regarding finances, it can lead to other problems. Money can help you enjoy your marriage and can also result in an abrupt end of the union. The discussion of money issue is very crucial before you get married and always maintain an open line of communication regarding finances in the marriage.

Financial Death in Marriages

$\mathcal{F}$inancial death in marriages adds to the stress that couples deal with daily. When fulfilling financial responsibilities in a marriage becomes an issue, stress level rises, arguments erupts, which can sometimes lead to physical abuse, words start to roll out (verbal abuse), holding grudges will become a norm, and divorce becomes imminent.

Why do couples let financial problems or stresses fly their family planes is an important question that couples need to answer. Many couples have allowed financial trouble to pilot their marriages. Financial death may occur sooner than expected if couples are not careful when planning their lives together. Finance in marriage is about the truth and trust but the responsibilities to prevent financial death or insufficiencies are equally shared by both men and women. The combination of old school idea when men and women believe that it is the responsibility of the man as the head of the household to provide for the family and the modern world financial obligations are usually the genesis of financial death in most marriages. Many couples have forgotten the importance of togetherness and teamwork in marriages but have allowed individualism and selfishness to define finances in their marriages. Although my heritage is from the so-called "old school" culture with "old school" ideas however; concerning my responsibility as the head of the household with financial obligations, my wife had to be included as a support.

Many husbands do not disclose their salaries to their spouses, and the reason is not quite clear. It seems it might be due to ego, culture, lack of trust, or other reasons. Most husbands are very secretive about how much they have in their pockets. Some men want their wives to believe they earn more money than they make, and some are ashamed their spouses earn more money than them. Financial stability starts with transparency and honesty in relationships.

In this modern society, most women have proven to be better home managers because of the ability to effectively multi-task by caring for children, keeping the house together, having full-time job or career, and still retain the title of a good wife without complaints. A woman will work better with money, penny-pinch, and better manage the household if she knows how much she is working with. I am also aware of some women or mothers who do not know how to set their priorities right and make a scale of preference, women who will pay large amounts for name-branded pocket books, get nails and hair done weekly, go on cruises whereas the electrical and telephone bills are yet to be paid. I am equally aware of women or mothers who will feed their children or families with fast foods and go to "soul food" restaurants with girlfriends, women who do not want their husbands to have any money in his pockets with the fear that he will have money to spend on other women or hangout with friends. Also, some women want to be in charge and have their husbands ask them for money to track his movements, actions, and expenses. Most women will work better with their husbands to ensure financial stability if they know what is on the table and what the spending range is. Understanding household finances and the honest contribution from both parties will sustain any marriage financially. The commitment of the involved parties is the ground rule to prevent financial death in marriages.

Financial death can be resuscitated with openness and trust. Marriage with no trust is already destroyed before its beginning. Prevention of financial death in marriage is a joint effort of the partners working together with trust and honesty to achieve stability. Achievement of financial stability is enforced by hard work, good planning, and determination to acquire desired results. Financial death in a marriage is not an excuse for separation or divorce because two heads are always better than one, and there is financial safety in numbers.

Emotional Death in Marriages

$\mathcal{T}$he Bible tells us and I believe that Jesus Christ the Son of God is the only one known to have died physically and risen back to life in history however; emotional death in marriage also can be resurrected. Marriage is like a brand new house in which you enjoy what you invest in it. When you upgrade a home, the value increases and lasts longer compared to a cheaper house without additional investments and lack of maintenance.

When emotional intimacy is lost in any marriage, the marriage becomes boring and cold. Loneliness becomes evident between the partners. Emotional connection is lost in such marriages, the couple starts to grow apart instead of together, both become unhappy, extramarital affairs becomes tempting and such marriage usually end in divorce. In many instances, couples often understand that there is a problem but do not know what the problem is. One partner in the marriage may be content with the way things are going and not willing to change things around while the other feels disconnected.

When emotional attachment becomes loose, it gives room to other breakdown in a marriage, attention is drawn from one's partner to the other, sexual desire in marriage is lost, appreciation for one's partner decreases, deception is introduced to the union, love dies, separation arrives, and divorce is the result. Emotional death can be avoided only when both parties recognizes and accept that their marriage is in trouble. Couples with difference of opinion or those not in agreement usually create barriers in a marriage, which can eventually lead to the couples growing farther apart.

Sexual deterioration is the most damaging aspect of emotional death in marriage. When emotional disconnection is in motion, partners engage in non-passionate love-making. It is almost impossible to be attracted to someone that you are not emotionally connected to, make passionate love to the person even if you are the best immense pretender. When emotions are disconnected, it is difficult to look your spouse in the eye and make passionate love to him or her, the way it is meant to be. Love-making will become more like a necessary chore that has to be done to keep your spouse quiet than an act of showing your partner that he or she is cherished, valued, and respected.

Signs of emotional death in marriages:

- Spouse not showing concern or interest in the daily events of their partners.

- Couples are no longer flirting with each other.

- Intense and open affection is decreased or lost.

- Couples stop touching each other with sexual intentions and desires.

- Spouse not willing to listen to their mate or cutting them off before their opinion is voiced out.

- Spouses cannot look at each other and feel fortunate to have each other.

- Spouses stop whispering to each other how much they love and appreciate one another.

- When spouses use abusive languages and vulgar names to address their partner.

- Spouse begins to feel better or superior to the other.

- Spouses cannot go to places together or even hold hands in public to show off the love for each other to the world.

- When spouses go the whole day not thinking about each other, about how much the absence of the other affects them, and how they look forward to going home to each other's arms.

Sexual intimacy is the product of emotional intimacy in any marriage but when emotional intimacy diminishes, sexual desires decreases, and it becomes less interesting. Men and women express their emotions in different ways therefore; spouses are to get themselves acquainted with who they are in love with. Knowledge of whom you love with regard to how they express their emotions and show affections is very important. It will help you to understand how to better approach the signs of imminent emotional death in a marriage.

It is very important that couples realize that building a marriage can be challenging however; sustaining a loving marriage is even harder. Marriage is like flowers, it needs pruning, and nurturing to keep it looking fresh. Emotional death in marriages can be resurrected only if the couples involved are willing and committed to rediscover each other, remembering why they fell in love at first, and remembering the good old memories of unending love promise they made to each other without limits.

Physical Death in Marriages

$\mathcal{M}$arriage is a personal, physical, psychological, emotional, and spiritual agreement entered into by two people witnessed and sealed by God as the third party. It is entered into by two people therefore, it takes one of the parties to end and annul the agreement. One way in which a marriage agreement can be broken as stated in traditional vows is "till death do us part."

The most obvious way marriage agreement can be broken is through the physical death of one spouse. The death of a person with whom we share intimacy and life with is one of the most devastating, distressing, and difficult experience anyone will ever have. It shakes the foundation of lives and throws live into chaos, which can lead to physical and psychological problems that can even hasten death. At the death of one spouse, life takes a different course that may be unimaginable to several people.

Some death take place gradually as in the case of a loved one with terminal disease while other deaths occur suddenly as in the case of loved one in fatal car accident, drowning incident, gunshot, or heart attack. Grief is the normal human reaction to loss, and it is a good process of healing, but unresolved grief usually has devastating effects on human lives. Grief is a subjective pain experienced by the surviving partner only and two people do not experience or express grief the same way. Grief mostly manifest itself in our physical appearances, doubts sinks in, and the surviving spouse becomes unsure if he or she will be able to live without the other spouse, be safe, take on new roles, still have close friends, and the question of what will happen next pops in, and so on. All these doubts create emotional stress and soon the body chemistry and function start to change. Sometimes, some people may experience shock, body numbness, and disbelief, Insomnia, weight loss, and lack of appetite also sets in.

People go through the same stages of grief differently such as denial, anger, bargaining, depression, and acceptance of fate. Spiritual people sometimes become angry with God, feeling disappointed and seeking answers why he did not let the "cup pass over." No one wants to lose a loved one but death is inevitable, and there are three aspect of physical death that no one knows. It remains a mystery to human knowledge and understanding what type of death a person will experience, where it will happen, and when it will occur. This is something no man can imagine or determine except by God Almighty.

When physical death of a spouse occurs, what is next is the question of remarriage, especially if the surviving spouse is still young and in the prime age. Death makes remarriage possible and acceptable because the surviving partner is free from the marriage vows between the individual and the deceased partner. Sometimes, family of the deceased spouse becomes angry with the surviving spouse's thought of remarriage. It could be that they feel the surviving spouse should not have a better life without their loved one or it could be the selfish thought of "why do you have to move on when we lost our loved one." Whatever it is, the surviving spouse is "FREE," and he or she may choose to remain alone or remarry to carry on the legacy of the deceased. Many have chosen to remarry to avert loneliness, get additional help raising the children of the deceased, for companionship, or to have children if none was born previously to the deceased. Whatever the surviving partner chooses to do, he or she has the right to live, move on, and be "FREE." One important fact to remember is to love, respects, cherish, and appreciate your spouse when you can because tomorrow is promised to no one. Always remember that physical death may arrive at any time to define your separation. Death is a must paid debt for everyone either married or not but the love and the memories shared when there was life will sustain the surviving partner.

Family Influence in Marriages

$\mathscr{F}$amily involvement is very important in marriages because they provide financial, physical, or emotional support to the newlyweds. Families are a part of our lives for several reasons one of which is the provision of continual support to members of their family. Family involvement could either be positive or negative, depending on the situation. Family involvement in the negative way is more observed than the positive contributions at any given time. Marriage is the abandonment of two worlds in order for a new one to start. It is not just about two people sharing their lives together but building a life together as one. Many young people, especially in this generation, believe that marriage is just between "me and my spouse" and are very quick to quote the Bible "a man shall leave his father and mother and shall cleave to his wife," but the reality is that marriage is not just between two people who want to be one but between two families coming together to form a new merger.

Family influence is greatly underestimated on new marriages, forgetting that we are products of our individual families. In any marriage, members of the family like mother, father, and siblings are the foundations of existence and continually will be a part of the persons' lives. The immediate family like the spouse and children represents the continuation of lives toward the future. For instance, once we get old, our children grow up, give birth to their children, and continue where we left off. There is no future without the past and people should neither neglect the foundation of life nor the immediate family. Starting a new life is great but the extended families should not be left out. The amount and the level of influence and control that families have over a marriage will depend on how much influence is permitted them. Newlyweds or married couples need to understand family influence and plan ahead on how to fortify their marriages in case of negative influence from families. Many families show support, love, and affection in different ways. If your extended family loves to shower you with gifts and praises for something extraordinary, your in-laws may not acknowledge such things as extraordinary. Some families will continually acknowledge your good deeds and be appreciative in years to come while some families will only say "thank you" to you once. Remember, you are just coming into the picture and to an unknown family you may be seen as an "intruder" because you are either coming to take his or her child away from him or her, share in his or her personal space, and leave him or her "maybe" abandoned. You will always be a child to your parents as long as they live regardless of your age. They are not sure if your intentions are to love or maltreat their family member. You are basically under the microscope until the air is clear and the more reason you cannot get upset when they act suspicious or ask questions that you find intrusive or offensive. Two families with two different ideas, two ways of life and opinion are coming together to start a new life. Always be receptive to your in-laws because one-day if things go "right" you will be in-law to somebody as well. Accepting your in-laws and family as part of your marriage may be advantageous as well as helping you to understand the "honey" you marry. Courting or dating as it is called in this part of the world is full of merriments and "lovey-dovey" blinding youngsters from the reality of what is to come. A good family influence will help you through difficult times when the reality hits your relationship or marriage and the "loving honey" start to show his or her true self.

Families are very important in marriages from a little family get together to giving support in time of difficulty. Family involvement is vital to marriage but the extent of involvement depends on how much you allow the family either positively or negatively. Be aware that someone raised and trained your "honey," fed your "baby," changed and clothed your "sweetie pie," grew with your "sweet heart," was once your "honey dew's" favorite, before he or she became your "BOO." Acknowledgement and recognition of members of the extended family as part of your marriage is crucial to the success of the marriage. Some couples do not have any family ties but to the majority that have good family involvement in their early stages in life, continual positive involvement will help move the new family forward.

Mother-In-Laws

For many years, mother-in-laws have been given bad names because of the few misunderstood or insensitive ones. There are many amazing mother in-laws out there that are sometimes more concerned about your welfare than their personal lives and their over-concern make it look as if they are intruding into your personal lives.

Some marriages do suffer because of mother-in-laws and due to lack of understanding or the unwillingness to co-habitat with the new addition in the family. Mother in-laws and their son or daughter-in-laws perceive each other as intruders. Most guys have had the opportunity to date many ladies off and on in their lifetime but their mothers have been in their lives throughout the dating era. Most men feel that they owe a great deal to their mothers who gave birth to them and possibly raised them single-handedly. Some mother-in-laws are guilty as charged because they hold what they went through while raising their children upon them and make them feel guilty. This often happens whenever the child cannot meet her demands or needs. Some mothers will let their children know-how much they meant to them and how they will not survive without them making their children obligated to come to their rescue all the time. Some mother-in-laws do try to control their children homes and family affairs and fail to respect the new family addition making it easier to categorize all mother-in-laws as one.

Mother-in-laws are a great deal and who can blame them for the belief "spell" they have over their children. It is very difficult sometimes not to feel as if you are walking through a metal detector at the airport when around some mother-in-laws because they perceive you as someone who wants to take their child away from them. Sometimes, many spouses have to prove himself or herself as a good person to the in-laws.

Many in-laws on the other hand, have forgotten that the happiness of their loved one is in alignment with the person he or she has trouble with. Having a good relationship with a son or daughter in-law is also part of having a strong family ties and forgetting that a joyful heart is good medicine for the body and a crushed spirit will cause trouble in the body even to your loved ones.

One starts to wonder sometimes if the in-laws truly love who they claim they love and if the love and attachment they have is due to what they derive from the person. When you claim to love someone, you love them unconditionally and if your family member chooses to spend his or her life with someone, the love that you claim to have, will have to be extended to the person who he or she has chosen. Compromise is the key because thinking that mother-in-laws will relinquish the child completely is impossible and to ask her to give up complete control of caretaking is a joke. She will always be part of you as no one like to feel like a loser, especially to someone that you see all the time over someone that you love and care for all your life. No mother-in-law will completely entrust all the care of their child to another person even to the spouse, at least until good trust is established or whenever the child in question is able to stand on his or her ground to let mother-in-law know that it is time to back off. It is also unfair to try to stop her from been concerned for her loved ones who she cared for all her life without any sensitivity for her feelings. Asking her to let you be the only "say" and "influential" person in her baby's life can be difficult forgetting that she can be a wonderful resource to you, helping you to understand who you marry. It is good to understand that it is sometimes difficult for mother-in-laws to accept that anyone is the best match for her children. Parents often believe their child is better than the chosen partner and can do better. Mother-in-laws are difficult to understand if patience is not exercised, but you will understand someday when you have to compete with a man or woman over your loved ones. If mother-in-laws are diligently, carefully, and respectfully approached the competitive attitude can be reduced and possibly eliminated. It is also a funny gesture that many sons and daughters-in-law display gentle, kind, and "I want to know your family attitude" while dating but as soon as the knot is tied, they feel empowered by the "union" and mother-in-laws are no longer welcome. Their presence becomes annoying and are perceived as intruders. This type of attitude raises eyebrows and alert mother-in-law that their son or daughter-in-law cannot be trusted. Feelings and involvement of parents toward their children, regardless of age and status is not like an electrical switch that you can turn on and off whenever it pleases you. Any marital issue with in-laws should be approached with care and humility without any hard feelings from all involved parties. Mother-in-laws can be useful guidance in the newly formed union, lead the way for a healthy marriage, and provide headway for a long-lasting partnership.

When to say "No"

$\mathcal{L}$ove as it is called comes in different ways, forms, and shapes. The love for your spouse is different from the love of parents. The love for children is different from that for siblings and in all honesty, all love categories listed can be expressed by one person in different ways. Spouse feeling a sense of jealousy over the love of parents and parent or sibling feeling ignored and abandoned over the expressed love for spouse is a common occurrence that have wrecked many marriages. Expression of love in this manner is separate but united as one.

Keeping family and spouse feeling separate is not difficult, especially for those truly in love but how do you prevent one from affecting the other is a million dollar question that needs answer. Do you have relationship with your family because of what you could provide for them, due to their selfishness and desire to keep you to themselves because of the fear of loosing most of the benefits they derive from you, or do they really love you for who you are. One may be certain that he or she is loved by their family members and relatives but one of the greatest selfishness discovered is the support of timid relatives in and out of our lives. Most spouses are sacrificed on the altar of duty to relatives. Relatives are sometimes fed and well taken care while malnutrition is seriously going on in their own homes. This is in the name of "family" and "goodness."

Spouses sometimes forget that what is not good for every member of a family is not good for the entire family and self-denial to support those who claim they cannot take care of themselves in the end hurts the people supported. Life is for growth and not to pamper, comfort, or pleasure. As Christianity is based on the teachings of our Lord Jesus Christ, one might question if letting relatives become predatory creatures is Biblical or not. There are some who will use the healthful doctrine of the Bible on you. Quotes like "be your brother's keeper'," "love one another," "provide for your brother's needs," "it is more blessed to give than to receive," "the parable of the Good Samaritan," and so on. However; people easily forget phrases like "love is considerate," "heaven helps those who help themselves," "treasure will be taken from those that have less and be added to those that have more," "each must give as he has decided in his heart not reluctantly or out of compulsion," "love does not insist on its own way," and so on. Many households have allowed relatives to place them in spiritual and traditional bondage. Many have used various phrases based on religion as well as tradition only when situations tend to be favorable to their needs.

When we decide to help someone else out of the little that we have, we need to determine if it is a need or a want. Some have more than you but are accustomed to taking from others to enrich themselves the way a parasite does. Many have deprived their immediate families of good or better things while caring for comfortable extended families and friends. Nothing should become an obligation merely because someone tells you it is. There is only one way to refuse a request with a clear conscience and that is to decide what relation to life the request in question bears. I do not see any harm in refusing to do what anyone asks if you only do it to please him and refusing with equal fortitude to endure any situation unless you see it as a cosmic responsibility. When a member of your family or friends seek for your assistance and insist that it is your responsibility to take care of him or her, imposing his or her needs upon others either directly or indirectly, you must remind him or her of what your primary responsibilities are, that is to your family. The world is full of people who will prefer to live as beggars having other people to cater for their needs and if you fail to stand on your ground, people are ready to walk over you in the process. Some family members are very appreciative while some are quick to forget your previous good gestures to them. Remember that every time you carry a healthy person, you weaken him more, and you are not helping him at all. Anyone who realize when to say "NO" and can say it pleasantly without causing embarrassments, hurt, and with no pride involvement has won half his battles in life. When you refuse to bear other's unnecessary problems be firm and honest about it. It is better to precipitate a crisis in the beginning than to have it in the end and do not forget you have the right to change your mind.

There is no opposition to helping others, especially those in need, and no disagreement in giving helping hands to those in need of assistance. You are in the position you are for a reason and you have been placed where you are to be a blessing unto others. The Holy books even support helping one another and letting our lights shine by giving to those in need, but for everything that we do in life, we must apply wisdom. I believe in divine intervention that if you fail to help others when you can, God will intervene, use someone else to accomplish His purpose. The point is that there must be a balance in rendering assistance to families, friends, and it must be done wisely. Do not deprive yourself and your family a good life just because you feel obligated to help others and in the process act foolish. A good charity begins in your home and saying "NO" when appropriate does not mean you love the individual "LESS."

A friend once shared his story with me about how he deprived his wife whose car needed some mechanical work and his children school supplies for a lesser amount of money, which he sent to his nephew. He discovered two months later that his nephew had lied, instead used the money he sent to pay "bride price" for a second wife. This type of situation can occur in a different form but apply knowledge and wisdom so that your assistance will not be a waste and not bring regret to you. Make sure you are supporting the right cause with your generosity and saying "NO" when appropriate will help you and others in question.

Secrets in Marriage

Secrecy in a marriage is like an ingredient used to prepare unhealthy marriage, which breeds dysfunctional family. Keeping secrets from your spouse is a time bomb waiting to explode. When a relationship is built on lies and dishonesty, lies, and deceits will follow to keep the lies alive. In a marriage, the two people who have come together will become one flesh, and one body, which makes lying and deceiving oneself unnecessary. Therefore, there should be no secrecy in a marriage. The word "secrecy" could be interpreted in many ways depending on who it benefits. We all have secret things that we do when we are alone, things that happened long time ago that we are not proud of such as fantasies or habits. Some of these secrets as we think are better to be kept secret for life. The way we look at our personal values depends on the things that we may decide to hide from our spouse and knowing when to share a secret or when to keep quiet aligns with individual conscience. Some say "honesty is the best policy" while some says you have the right to your privacy. Considering both sayings requires better understanding of marriage and its entity as two people coming together to share their love, affection, and space with no boundaries. Having an e-mail, cell phone, or bank accounts are examples of privacy rights but keeping the passwords from your spouse is a sign of "secrecy" in marriage. Everyone have rights to acquire wealth and do things as he or she pleases but once married, there is no more "me or I," which means no more secrets and no more individual decisions. When spouses decide to keep individual dealings as secrets, they are preparing themselves for a long marital heartache. Some believe it is acceptable in the beginning of the relationship to have privacy but as years go by; it becomes problematic in their relationships. This is so because one party becomes suspicious of the other while the other enjoys the freedom, and this makes it difficult to reverse the situation after several years of marriage with separate lifestyle. Cell phones, e-mails, social networks are all convenient and tempting technologies of our time that makes contacting others easier, but it can also become a tool used to keep secrets from your spouse. Relationships and marriages are built on trust, and it is almost impossible to have a true marriage without trusting one another. Some people keep secrets about their income, some about their spending, and some about their savings. Lies, deceits, and secrets come in different forms and having a consistent behavior of intentional secrecy is a sick behavior that can become a breaking ground for the building of a dysfunctional relationship.

Some professions are excused from openness and as we understand the nature of these professions, keeping secrets may be a useful tool to be efficient. Clergy, therapists, counselors, law enforcements, doctors, nurses are some professions requiring having good relationship with people built on trust and confidence. Once this trust is violated, it is almost impossible to regain it back. If members of these professions discuss their client issues with their spouses when he or she is not involve in the matter, it becomes a violation of the client's right to his or her privacy.

Many people get involved in new relationships with baggage, disappointments, and distrust from the previous involvements and have held it within for so long that it becomes difficult to trust someone else for the fear of being hurt all over again.

For the new relationship to progress, people may need to open the unfortunate baggage for the spouse to unpack all the disappointments and trust violations so that it does not infect the current relationship like a disease. Keeping secrets in a marriage can be compared to a deadly poison in which little amount can be lethal. It is good to think about the ideal way to confess about the past to your partner in a way that it will not be a continual problem in the marriage or relationship. You may be criticized for your confession and remember that you are doing it not just for your partner but for yourself as well because being clean and honest will enhance your sanity and peace of mind. A secret free marriage sacrifices individual's concerns for the utmost well being of the union. A healthy marriage is one in which the partners involved are not holding out on anything from one another and a good marriage or relationship is built on honesty and transparency.

Marriage Advice

- ➤ Enjoy the warmth and affection you give each other.

- ➤ Trust in the feelings and dreams you share with each other.

- ➤ Always celebrate the love that brought you together and which will carry you through all the days to come.

Ladies

- Always remember your thoughts the very first day you met him.

- Respect his leadership as the head of the house.

- Do not undermine his authority.

- Give him your full support.

- Honor him and accept him for who he is.

- Do not allow any third party (except God) to interfere in your relationship.

Gentlemen

- If you have to walk away, walk away from confrontation and NOT your family.

- If you have to leave anything, let it be bachelor's lifestyles.

- If you have to punch or kick, please punch and kick bad habits Not your wife.

- Be committed to your relationship.

- Take a very good care of your family.

- Marriage can be tested but instead of looking for space, look for God's grace

To Both

- If you have to cheat at all, cheat death.

- If you have to love, love God who give and take because everything beautiful begins with love.

- Love each other without reservation.

- Take care of yourself Physically,

- Take care of each other Emotionally.

- Live a happy and healthy life.